SUICIDE:

Small Group Study Guide

A ministry resource for churches to help
people who have lost someone to suicide

Dr. Thomas Perchitti

RIVER BIRCH PRESS

Daphne, Alabama

ISBN 978-1-956365-47-4 (print)
ISBN 978-1-956365-48-1 (e-book)

For Worldwide Distribution
Printed in the U.S.A.

River Birch Press
P.O. Box 868, Daphne, AL 36526

Table of Contents

Introduction

*A ministry resource for churches to help people
who have lost someone to suicide*

For many of us suicide is an "it happens to other people"
event. Like the fire that burned down an empty warehouse on
the other side of town, we hear about it and quickly filter it
out of our minds. The fact is that:

Suicide is an epidemic in our nation and our world.
According to the World Health Organization, close to
800,000 people die due to suicide every year, this is one
person every 40 seconds. Suicide is a global phenome-
non and occurs throughout the lifespan. Effective and
evidence-based interventions can be implemented at
population, sub-population and individual levels to
prevent suicide and suicide attempts. There are indica-
tions that for each adult who died by suicide there may
have been more than 20 others attempting suicide.[1]

As you are reading this in your church, your small group,
or other ministry-related setting, think about the fact that two
or more people have just died by suicide. That is mind-blowing,
and people need the Lord everywhere at all times! When these
atrocities occur, that means many more people who loved and
knew those people intimately and relationally have lost a loved
one to suicide. You may be thinking, *well, this is someone else's
problem, there are internet and phone based services and hotlines
and mental health facilities and workers specialized to deal with
this*, and you would be correct.

---

[1] https://www.who.int/mental_health/prevention/suicide/suicideprevent/en/

However, the most pressing questions, issues, fears, and torments for these survivors (many of whom will be thinking about suicide as well) are spiritual. That's right! Related to things beyond this life, concerning eternal destinations, judgment, and damnation. That is why this resource is needed now more than ever for you and your church. We all need to be more aware, better equipped, and ministry-minded in order to be able to help these people who have questions that only the Word of God can effectively answer. This ministry is to specifically help those people who are all around us!

In this ministry guidebook, we will journey through the Scriptures and find the answers to the most commonly held spiritual questions that people have when someone they know and love has died by suicide. We will explore the thoughts and feelings of clergy concerning suicide and its effects. All of this material is presented in book form in my book *Suicide Unforgivable? A Grace Manual for Those Who Have Lost a Loved One to Suicide.* In it we will learn how to properly reference the Bible when speaking with a person who has lost a loved one to suicide. We will also be challenged to be intentionally ministry minded with people who have lost a loved one to suicide. We leave this section with a Bible verse to ponder as we know that there is nothing to be said in this guide book which condones suicide in any form. Life is a gift from God and is precious and needs to be lived as such.

The Psalmist praises his maker in Psalm 139:14:

I praise you because I am fearfully and wonderfully made; your works are wonderful, I know that full well.

Session One

What are the spiritual questions that people who have lost a loved one to suicide might ask?

1. Is my loved one in hell?
2. Is suicide the "unforgivable sin"?
3. How can the church help me?
4. Where can I find hope?
5. Is it my fault?

As you ponder these questions, please attempt to put yourself in the shoes of someone who has lost a loved one to suicide (if you have lost a loved one, perhaps you have asked one or more of these questions) and who is desperately looking for spiritual answers (which are often provided by movies, television, social-media, blogs and friends and family) and have come up empty. When these individuals hear about suicide and its spiritual implications from culture and other sources (apart from the Scriptures), it is easy to see that they believe untruths, they suffer from isolation, and oftentimes have depression and suicidal thoughts themselves. They need biblical answers to their questions, and together we are going to learn how we can provide them for them.

Remember, you are not a mental health professional so if someone ever tells you that they are thinking about doing harm to themselves, you need to call 911 and get them help immediately.

By the end of this guidebook you will be better equipped as an individual, a church congregation, a pastor, etc., to provide biblical answers and minister to this population of individuals who so desperately need help.

Identity moment: Throughout the guidebook, you will find a title at the end of some chapters which is labeled specifically as follows:

Identity Moment

Identity Moments will provide you with clarity about what you have read and a summation of the contents of the words of Scripture through which you can gain insight to help you.

Let's talk about the first question...it is a doozy!

Question #1: Is my loved one in hell?

- Defining the unforgivable from a biblical point of view concerning human life begins with the law expressing that murder is prohibited.

- Knowing that Jesus' death and resurrection provided the means of grace through which people could be forgiven and have eternal life in heaven with God through sole faith (trust) in Him provides assurance for anyone.

  1 Peter 1:3: *Blessed be the God and Father of our Lord Jesus Christ, who according to His abundant mercy has begotten us again to a living hope through the resurrection of Jesus Christ from the dead.*

- In Exodus 20:13, it states simply, "You shall not murder." This command is repeated in Deuteronomy 5:17. Earlier in the Bible, in Genesis 9:6, God says, "Whoever sheds man's blood, by man his blood shall be shed, for in the image of God He made man." In Leviticus 24:17 (NASB) it states, "If a man takes the life of any human being, he shall surely be put to death."

- It is interesting that nowhere in the Bible is the word "suicide" specifically used, although there are a few occurrences of suicides recorded in the Scriptures (1 Samuel 31:3-5; 2 Samuel 17:23; Judges 9:50-55; Judges 16:29-30; 1 Kings 16:15-20; Matthew 27:5).

When speaking of hell and suicide, take a moment in your group to read these passages out loud and discuss them, asking simple, relevant questions: Questions that come from what the passages say (not speculative) and are interpretive (not merely observations which reiterate the passage). Questions which are answered by staying with the information provided in the passage (not doctrinal, not denominational). Questions which view the truth of the verses in the passage and are not outside of its theme or context. Questions which lead to further examination and explanation of the passage and subject through the chapter, book and rest of the Bible.

For example: we read in 2 Corinthians 5:9-10 that,

Therefore we make it our aim, whether present or absent, to be well pleasing to Him. For we must all appear before the judgment seat of Christ, that each one may receive the things done in the body, according to what he has done, whether good or bad.

A good question about this passage might be, "How are we going to be judged by Christ?" This is simple, relevant and leads to further examination and explanation of the passage and subject. The answer comes from the passage "for the things we have done in the body (while living on earth) good and bad."

Regarding hell, the Word of God is clear: John 3:17 says, "For God did not send His Son into the world to condemn the world; but that the world through Him might be saved." The word *condemn* there means "to judge, to try as in a judicial manner." He sent not His Son into the world to condemn it, "but that the world through him might be saved." The Greek word *sozo* literally means "eternal salvation granted by God." It is interesting in this passage that Zoe life—"spiritual life"— is combined with eternal salvation in these verses.

4

Now notice verse 18: "He who believes in Him is not condemned; but he who does not believe is condemned already, because he has not believed in the name of the only begotten Son of God." Notice that it says "believeth on Him" in that verse. *To believe in* is to hold as the object of faith. *To believe on* is to trust, to place full confidence in, to rest upon with faith.

To believe on Him is to be *not condemned*, the same word for condemn used earlier, which means "to judge, to try in a judicial manner." It is specifically related to **eternal condemnation** because the previous verses and contexts are talking about eternal life and not perishing and being saved, so we must conclude that this condemnation is an eternal condemnation of one who is not saved. They are condemned already... why? Because they have not believed in the name of the only begotten Son of God. The Greek word for "belief" is *pistis*, which means "confidence" or "trust." The root word is *peitho*, which means "to convince." Therefore, belief is to place one's trust in God's truth. A person who believes is one who takes God at His Word and trusts in Him for salvation.

A person (anyone) who has placed their trust and faith in Jesus is saved! So the clear-cut answer to the question, "Is my loved one in hell?" is this: **If they have placed their trust and faith in Jesus they cannot be in hell, or the Word of God is not true and reliable.**

This truth can provide someone who has lost a loved one to suicide with the **assurance** that they will see their loved one again if they passed on and had faith in the risen Lord! Assurance is something we all seek, something we look for in doing daily things. When we go to the grocery store to pick up meat, we want to be assured that is not going to poison us. When we get in the car, we want to be assured that it is going to start. There are so many things in life we might take for granted, but believe me, being assured is something that breeds confidence. It lets us know something is reliable in a world filled with so many unreliable things.

Discussion Notes

1. What can I learn from these passages about suicide?

    1 Samuel 31:3-5   Judges 16:29-30
    2 Samuel 17:23   I Kings 16:15-20
    Judges 9:50-55   Matthew 27:5

    _____

    _____

    _____

2. What is the criterion for someone being saved?

    _____

    _____

    _____

3. How can I share these truths and provide assurance for others?

    _____

    _____

    _____

Assurance Verses

Acts 2:32: This Jesus God has raised up, of which we are all witnesses.

Acts 17:31: Because He has appointed a day on which He will judge the world in righteousness by the Man whom He has ordained. He has given assurance of this to all by raising Him from the dead."

Acts 1:3: To whom He also presented Himself alive after His suffering by many infallible proofs, being seen by them during forty days and speaking of the things pertaining to the kingdom of God.

Acts 1:22: Beginning from the baptism of John to that day when He was taken up from us, one of these must become a witness with us of His resurrection.

Acts 10:39-41: And we are witnesses of all things which He did both in the land of the Jews and in Jerusalem, whom they killed by hanging on a tree. Him God raised up on the third day, and showed Him openly, not to all the people, but to witnesses chosen before by God, even to us who ate and drank with Him after He arose from the dead.

Acts 13:30-31: But God raised Him from the dead. He was seen for many days by those who came up with Him from Galilee to Jerusalem, who are His witnesses to the people.

Romans 1:4: And declared to be the Son of God with power according to the Spirit of holiness, by the resurrection from the dead.

1 Corinthians 15:3-7: For I delivered to you first of all that which I also received: that Christ died for our sins according to the Scriptures, and that He was buried, and that He rose again the third day according to the Scriptures, and that He was seen by Cephas, then by the twelve. After that He was seen by over five hundred brethren at once, of whom the greater part remain to the present, but some have fallen asleep. After that He was seen by James, then by all the apostles.

1 Peter 1:3: Blessed be the God and Father of our Lord Jesus

Christ, who according to His abundant mercy has begotten us again to a living hope through the resurrection of Jesus Christ from the dead.

Group Discussion

1. How can we more effectively witness to people who have lost a loved one to suicide in our church? Our community?

2. Do the verses about suicide show us anything which we can use in helping others?

3. How do the verses on assurance impact me personally and how can this effectively be translated into real-world application in my life so I can use them to minister to people who have lost loved ones to suicide?

Identity Moment

If Jesus is your Savior, then as you live and breathe right now, you are assured of eternal life!

Session Two

Question #2: Is suicide the "unforgivable sin"?

Jesus states "Truly I say to you, all sins will be forgiven the sons of men, and whatever blasphemies they utter" Mark 3:28 (cf. Matthew 12:31-32; Luke 12:10).

This question in varying forms has been asked by many who have dealt with suicide in their families: **"Where is my loved one?"** This is overwhelmingly the first question asked by bereaved family members to clergy members as they wish to know about the eternal state of their loved ones. These are understandable questions for persons who are suffering with the loss of their loved ones to suicide.

The *Anchor Yale Bible Dictionary* begins its treatment of suicide with the following:

> The taking of one's own life is always morally problematic. Religiously motivated suicide is particularly sensitive as an issue in the history of Jewish and Christian thought, and is closely related to issues of martyrdom and redemptive suffering generally.[1]

It is further of interest that, "One of the difficulties Augustine and later theologians had in defending their condemnation of suicide is that neither the Hebrew Bible nor the New Testament explicitly prohibits the act."[2] Defining the **unforgivable** from a biblical point of view concerning human life begins with the law expressing that **murder** is prohibited.

[1] A. J. Droge, "Suicide," ed. David Noel Freedman, *The Anchor Yale Bible Dictionary* (New York: Doubleday, 1992), 225.
[2] Ibid., 227.

Exodus 20:13 states simply, "You shall not murder." This command is repeated in Deuteronomy 5:17. Earlier in the Bible, God says, "Whoever sheds man's blood, by man his blood shall be shed, for in the image of God He made man."[3] Leviticus 24:17 (NASB) states, "If a man takes the life of any human being, he shall surely be put to death."

Many people say that murder is not directly related to suicide. Others say that suicide is defined as "self-murder." It is interesting that nowhere in the Bible is the word "suicide" specifically used, although there are a few occurrences of suicides recorded in the Scriptures.

One of the first recorded examples occurs in 1 Samuel 31:3-5, where the death of King Saul and his armor-bearer are recorded. Here it says:

> *The fighting grew fierce around Saul, and when the archers overtook him, they wounded him critically. Saul said to his armor-bearer, "Draw your sword and run me through, or these uncircumcised fellows will come and run me through and abuse me." But his armor-bearer was terrified and would not do it; so Saul took his own sword and fell on it. When the armor-bearer saw that Saul was dead, he too fell on his sword and died with him.*

Later on 2 Samuel 17:23 indicates,

> *When Ahithophel saw that his advice had not been followed, he saddled his donkey and set out for his house in his hometown. He put his house in order and then hanged himself. So he died and was buried in his father's tomb.*

In Judges 9:50-55, King Abimelech, who was injured by having a millstone dropped on his head by a woman, had his

---

[3] Genesis 9:6.

personal armor-bearer then kill him so that it could not be said that a woman killed him.

The next recorded example occurs when Samson destroys himself and the Philistines in Judges 16:29-30:

> *Then Samson reached toward the two central pillars on which the temple stood. Bracing himself against them, his right hand on the one and his left hand on the other, Samson said, "Let me die with the Philistines!" Then he pushed with all his might, and down came the temple on the rulers and all the people in it. Thus he killed many more when he died than while he lived.*

Another king named Zimri set his palace on fire around him when he saw that he was about to be overtaken by his enemies. This instance is recorded in 1 Kings 16:15-20. And perhaps the most famous case of suicide recorded in the Scriptures is of the betrayer Judas Iscariot, who hanged himself as recorded in the Gospel of Matthew 27:5.

These are all of the instances recorded in Scriptures regarding historical persons who died at their own hand or commanded someone to take their life. It is interesting that only Judas Iscariot (who was referred to as the "Son of Perdition" in John's Gospel prior to taking his life)[4] is strongly believed to be unrepentant and unsaved. In no other example in the Scriptures is a suicide and the victim thereof said to be in danger of eternal damnation.

Given the biblical reference to a sin which cannot be forgiven, it is logical that if suicide was that sin, it would have been mentioned in one of the examples listed above or somewhere else in the biblical texts.

---

4 John 17:12.

Unforgiven?

So what is unforgivable according to Christ for all ages (into eternity not capable of being purged in any way)? If, indeed Jesus paid the payment for all sins, how can there be an unforgivable sin? We hearken back to Mark 3:22-30 (NASB):

The scribes who came down from Jerusalem were saying, "He is possessed by Beelzebul," and "He casts out the demons by the ruler of the demons." And He called them to Himself and began speaking to them in parables, "How can Satan cast out Satan? If a kingdom is divided against itself, that kingdom cannot stand. If a house is divided against itself, that house will not be able to stand. If Satan has risen up against himself and is divided, he cannot stand, but he is finished! But no one can enter the strong man's house and plunder his property unless he first binds the strong man, and then he will plunder his house.

"Truly I say to you, all sins shall be forgiven the sons of men, and whatever blasphemies they utter; But whoever blasphemes against the Holy Spirit never has forgiveness, but is guilty of an eternal sin—because they were saying, "He has an unclean spirit."

If you notice specifically in verse 28, it says, "Truly I say to you, all sins shall be forgiven the sons of men, and whatever blasphemies they utter." We must take into consideration who was speaking, under what authority they are speaking, and what they are saying. Jesus is speaking, He is speaking in the authority of God, and He is saying without hesitation that all sins will be forgiven, even blasphemies against God. So that means He understood that He would pay for sins so that sin is no longer the issue; it would be dealt with by His blood at Calvary. Hence, He is the propitiation for the sins of the world. This is done by His authority as God in flesh; it is done by His word.

Further, we can state that the people who are lost and going into the Lake of Fire have had their sins paid for; however, they have not personally applied the blood of Christ by faith. This is indeed the unforgivable sin: blasphemy of the Holy Spirit as it is the Spirit who testifies to the reality of the Christ, and none can say Jesus is Lord but by the Holy Spirit.

This shows that the people who stand before Christ at the Great White Throne Judgment have a hardened heart. So hardened in their rejection of Jesus as God's true Savior and Messiah, they attribute to the devil the works of the Holy Spirit done in and through Jesus. They will never be forgiven as they are guilty of an eternal (unending through eternity with no changing), ongoing sin. They are, in essence, rejecting the only sacrifice for their sins and have no other sacrifice ("For if we sin willfully after we have received the knowledge of the truth, there no longer remains a sacrifice for sins.")[5] because He offered it once and for all!

This is a willful and deliberate rejection that is ongoing in the person who denies the testimony of the Holy Spirit which reveals the truth about Jesus, namely, that He is the Son of God, and all of the subsequent truths surrounding Himself, His nature, and His works. This ongoing, willful and deliberate rejection of Christ makes the one who bore the sins of the person who does this of no effect. In other words, His payment for sin is not applicable to their lives. So they must stand before God at the Great White Throne Judgment on the merit of

[5] Hebrews 10:26.

their own works, which are as filthy rags before the Lord, and not on the merit of the saving grace of God in Christ.

One commentator puts it this way concerning the fixed nature detailed in the passage: "The use of the imperfect tense of the verb in the explanatory note, 'because they were saying that he is possessed,' implies repetition and a fixed attitude of mind, the tokens of callousness which brought the scribes to the brink of unforgivable blasphemy."[6] What this is saying is that the individual who commits blasphemy of the Holy Spirit or does not recognize the testimony of the Holy Spirit regarding Christ and His work is deserving of eternal condemnation.

This eternal condemnation is directly referring to the eternal judgment that will come in the future when Jesus returns as King of Kings and Lord of Lords, and judges in accordance with what has been revealed in Scripture. If anyone in this present age denies the Holy Spirit as He testifies to the truth about who Jesus is and what He did for them in dying on the cross for their sins, being buried in a tomb and being resurrected, that person is in danger of eternal judgment. Putting it simply, rejecting the authentic message of the Word, which is testified to by the Holy Spirit about Jesus Christ, and rejecting Him completely as Savior, puts a person into eternal condemnation.

Suicide

Suicide is not the "unforgivable sin." Blasphemy of the Holy Spirit is the unpardonable and unforgivable sin. If a person has accepted Jesus Christ as their Savior, then they are not in danger of committing the unforgivable sin. Throughout the

---

[6] William L. Lane, *The Gospel of Mark* (Wm. B. Eerdmans Publishing, 1974), 146.

ages and throughout the perceptions and sometimes teachings of religion, religious leaders, philosophers, and others, suicide has been mistakenly defined as something that is not pardonable by God. The clergy interviewed indicated that it was not their place to judge, and that they believed that suicide was forgivable by God.

One clergy member indicated,

> Sometimes, they just simply want to confess their sin, not necessarily that specific thing, but they need to be reminded of the love of Jesus and His forgiveness. It is not the unforgivable sin. That's a sin against the Holy Spirit.

Another said,

> The story about Jesus and His love for you and for all of us, to the extent that He did what He did. He took our sins in His body and the cross; all you have to do is reach out for that forgiveness and claim it as your own. He was having severe difficulty with that. I just lightly touched his arm in a plea, just please, just reach out and say, "Forgive me."

The clergy referenced the common belief that suicide is a sin because it was the violation of God's commands; however, it was not the unforgivable sin, and further, the clergy indicated that suicide could be forgiven and that cases had to be examined individually. One of the clergy members indicated that, while they were in the middle of counseling a depressed individual about forgiveness,

> We went to Jesus in prayer, we went to Him in study, and I just kept reminding her how much Christ loved her, that He died for all sin, not the pretty ones, and

that yes, there can be love, forgiveness and peace again."

When speaking directly about the afterlife, one of the religious professionals said,

> I would more or less lean on the mercy of God and say, "Well, I can't tell you the answer, but I do know that the Lord is merciful, loving, and we don't know what happened in their last moments. But we certainly hope that they are there with the Lord, and insofar as they trusted in Christ, they are with the Lord."

The implication of this is that even when a person is on the cusp of suicide, they may be seeking forgiveness from God through Christ.

A story is detailed that occurred several years ago about an individual who was jumping off a bridge. Whether it is fact or fiction, I do not know. The story goes this way: The person was falling down in the air after jumping off of a high bridge, but as they were falling they began to cry out to Jesus to save them and forgive them. It is curious—if they were committing suicide, how do people know what they were saying as they were falling? They survived. In their statement following this incident, they indicated that while they were in the air they called out to Jesus for salvation. They are now apparently a Christian and are still living.

While there may be other stories of this nature, the point is obvious: Even when a person is about to or is attempting to commit suicide, we do not know if they are calling on Jesus for forgiveness. We may not know how people in their last moments on this earth may be calling on Christ for salvation, so we cannot make hasty assumptions about their spiritual standing before God.

Look at the following passage in Luke 23:40-43 (KJV):

But the other answering rebuked him, saying, Dost not thou fear God, seeing thou art in the same condemnation? And we indeed justly; for we receive the due reward of our deeds: but this man hath done nothing amiss. And he said unto Jesus, Lord, remember me when thou comest into thy kingdom. And Jesus said unto him, Verily I say unto thee, Today shalt thou be with me in paradise.

The man was about to die, and in his last moments called on the Lord. This man was one who:

1. Glorified God in his death moment.

2. Refrained from casting judgment on someone (Jesus) who was in the same position (on a cross) as he was, though being completely innocent.

3. Openly admitted that he was guilty of the crime he had committed.

4. Freely confessed/addressed Jesus Christ as Lord.

5. Received God's grace in Jesus Christ.

The Bible is clear that "Everyone who calls on the name of the Lord will be saved."[7] This is further backed by one of the clergy, who indicated that, "We would never say that someone who has committed suicide is condemned to Hell, for example, or is never going to achieve salvation, because we just don't know. The Lord is gracious!" Gracious, indeed!

---

[7] Romans 10:13.

Discussion Notes

1. What can I learn from this passage and others mentioned about the unforgivable sin? Mark 3:22-30:

_____

_____

_____

2. What is the criterion for someone to have committed the unforgivable, eternal sin?

_____

_____

_____

3. Is suicide the unforgivable sin?

_____

_____

_____

Group Discussion

1. How can we better get the truth out, that the Bible is clear their loved one has not committed the "unforgivable sin"?

2. Do the verses about people who have committed suicide recorded in the Bible show us anything that we can use in helping others understand the grace of God?

3. How can knowing the truth about the unforgivable sin help us to minister to this population whom has been told lies (and believes them) by religion, culture and even members of their circle of family and friends?

Identity Moment

**You are human! Created in God's image and He loves you!
Your identity is not formed by the failures of others;
it is formed in Christ!**

Session Three

Question #3: How can the church help me?

This is why we are here! We have resources that are distinct and necessary to help this population from God Himself! How do we mobilize them? Being there is a great place to start! Ministry of presence is powerful!

What exactly is a **"ministry of presence"**? It can narrowly be defined as "being there for someone when they need you." As related to the clergy, it is their being there for others as religious subject matter experts, spiritual guides and advisors, friends, compassionate and empathetic listeners, and genuinely concerned fellow humans. Needless to say, when I am down, when I feel stressed, when I have doubt and a level of fear or anxiety, someone being there for me and with me (even though they might not need to speak much) makes all the difference.

We will define it now as something essential for people dealing with loss and depression in any form. The clergy interviewed feel that through ministry of presence, being proactive in counseling situations and providing support and encouragement for persons suffering with suicidal ramifications are necessary and helpful to those individuals. You do not have to be a professional counselor or pastor to be there for another human being!

Through ministry of presence you are there as a believer, a blood-bought, sanctified, child of God through Christ, a living witness to the power of the cross and Christ to the person who needs it. Besides that you will be prepared with biblical knowledge and resources along with your church-organized activities so that you can help this person realize that through you and through the church they can have support and help that can't be found elsewhere!

In speaking with numerous clergy members, I found that the discussions centered on their realities involving their levels of training in suicide prevention as related to their faith. Their beliefs about labeling suicide a sin, yet being non-judgmental towards victims of suicide and helping families cope, were very important to them. All the clergy interviewed viewed suicide prevention as related to their denominational and religious backgrounds and as something which they could engage with spiritual resources (such as prayer, sacramental observances, shepherding-like guidance, integration into a religious community, and demonstrations of compassion and love).

Clergy members view their roles in the suicide prevention process as extending to religious-based counseling and just "being present" for persons suffering with depression and the families of suicide victims. While the clergy understand the limitations of their levels of training and overall suicide prevention experience, they expressed a clear understanding of the necessity of linking, referring, and collaborating with mental health professionals.

A genuine exhibition of empathy was exhibited by clergy members as they often realized their own shortcomings. In this regard, they lacked confidence in their abilities to effectively deal with individuals coming to them with suicidal problems. Sadness and genuine displays of love were echoed throughout the interviews with the clergy as they pondered suicide and its effects on communities, families, and society overall.

The clergy displayed a level of confidence in helping persons with suicidal difficulties through their faith tenets. Clergy members believe that they could privately counsel depressed individuals and provide spiritual advice rooted in the teachings of their faith traditions. Beyond that, the clergy confirmed that they would defer to mental health personnel once the scope of the counseling went beyond their level of training.

This is consistent with literature that is available, which details improvements in the clergy's overall abilities to identify and refer out persons who are experiencing active suicidal ideations, with a further understanding of the distinctions between active and passive suicidal gestures. The clergy often viewed suicidal thoughts as a product of spiritual issues but also understood that mental illness and emotional distress are legitimate sources of suicidal ideations.

Clergy members hold to the notion that, in their roles as priests and pastors, they are subject matter experts on issues related to life and death, as portrayed within their faith traditions. The notion that life is sacred, coupled with the understanding that suicide itself may not necessarily be the willful voluntary act of a person suffering with mental illness, was acknowledged and widely agreed with by the clergy.

They will help you when culture says just forget about it and keep going. They will help you understand matters of the spirit. They will provide you with comforting words which they deeply believe and feel in order to guide you through this and other tragedies. Although the clergy cannot diagnose, assess, nor actively treat persons suffering with active suicidal ideations, clergy members believe that they have a responsibility to help these individuals in a manner consistent with their faith traditions to the utmost of their abilities.

These perceptions and realizations on the part of the clergy may open up avenues of further involvement for them in mental health settings. In turn, it could allow for a co-joining with mental health professionals to provide a holistic level of care and treatment for persons needing it, which would include counsel and support for grieving family members and friends.

Your church, through your leaders, can identify resources which you can use to help you to:

1) Seek out people in your community who have lost loved ones to suicide, through outlets such as: social media, obituaries, local support groups concerning depression, AA/NA groups in your area, word of mouth and many others.

2) Plan events at your church specifically, which invite this population group to come and be a part of—hosting through community partnerships (such as the Red Cross, etc.) events at your church that deal directly with suicide and its effects. Plan a weekend conference/workshop where speakers come and offer related trainings to promote awareness, for instance.

3) Have leadership seek out faith-based resources dealing with depression and suicide—peruse the internet for pamphlets, training, and other materials that will help to increase awareness, knowledge, and ministerial support for the church members and people in your local community.

4) Identify people in your congregation who work in related fields—Mental health professionals, health care workers, and counselors of all types are resources you may have seated Sunday after Sunday in your church.

5) Set up prayer warriors specifically to pray as you minister to this population.

We have resources, and people who have lost loved ones to suicide need church-based resources to change their lives! It is clear that through prayer, we can provide and demonstrate love; however, people need resources, and the resources that could be offered through the churches to the bereaved are plenteous and needed. One clergy member remarked, "With the breakdown of the family, people are not learning how to love and how to receive love and how to give love. The church can provide support in this area." Regardless of their religious affiliation or their experience levels as clergy, all of them unanimously indicated that they and the community as a whole would benefit from increased training opportunities and workshops, which could then be filtered into the lives of the bereaved so they could be helped.

Lastly, a key factor in helping the bereaved is the infusion of hope and meaning into their lives, which can be provided through communion with Christ. For the clergy, this meant being present with those suffering individuals in a manner far exceeding their other support networks. One stated, "And the touch startled him, that a chaplain would even touch him and in his awful, awful state, it just stunned him and he was comforted."

Another indicated, "I was with them and that mattered to them. I tried to assure them that God is present in their lives, even ahead of the steps that they are taking, that God is already in their future, and that they needn't be afraid, but they could trust in that." What it means for you and I is that through the gospel, only through Christ, can people be renewed spiritually (reconciled to God) and live lives filled with hope and meaning like ours! More on this in the next session!

Discussion Notes

1. What immediate resources can we identify that our within our church right now to help the bereaved? What resources are we lacking? How can we begin to incorporate the needed resources into the life blood of our church?

_____

_____

_____

2. What is the ministry of presence? How can I practice it? Are there any personal hindrances in my life which might prevent me from using it?

_____

_____

_____

3. How does the hope and meaning I have in Christ impact my own life when I feel depressed or down? How can I relate this to others who are grieving and depressed?

_____

_____

_____

Bible Verses Regarding Reconciliation to God
A Broken Relationship through Sin Brings Alienation from God.

Isaiah 59:2: But your iniquities have separated you from your God; And your sins have hidden His face from you, So that He will not hear.

Genesis 3:23-24: Therefore the Lord God sent him out of the garden of Eden to till the ground from which he was taken. So He drove out the man; and He placed cherubim at the east of the garden of Eden, and a flaming sword which turned every way, to guard the way to the tree of life.

Genesis 4:13-14: And Cain said to the Lord, "My punishment is greater than I can bear! Surely You have driven me out this day from the face of the ground; I shall be hidden from Your face; I shall be a fugitive and a vagabond on the earth, and it will happen that anyone who finds me will kill me."

Isaiah 48:22: "There is no peace," says the Lord, "for the wicked."

Isaiah 64:7: And there is no one who calls on Your name, Who stirs himself up to take hold of You; For You have hidden Your face from us, And have consumed us because of our iniquities.

Jeremiah 33:5: "They come to fight with the Chaldeans, but only to fill their places with the dead bodies of men whom I will slay in My anger and My fury, all for whose wickedness I have hidden My face from this city."

Luke 18:13: And the tax collector, standing afar off, would not so much as raise his eyes to heaven, but beat his breast, saying, 'God, be merciful to me a sinner!'

Romans 5:10: For if when we were enemies we were reconciled to God through the death of His Son, much more, having been reconciled, we shall be saved by His life.

Romans 8:7: Because the carnal mind is enmity against God; for it is not subject to the law of God, nor indeed can be.

Ephesians 2:1-3: And you He made alive, who were dead in trespasses and sins, in which you once walked according to the course of this world, according to the prince of the power of the air, the spirit who now works in the sons of disobedience, among whom also we all once conducted ourselves in the lusts of our flesh, fulfilling the desires of the flesh and of the mind, and were by nature children of wrath, just as the others.

Ephesians 2:12: That at that time you were without Christ, being aliens from the commonwealth of Israel and strangers from the covenants of promise, having no hope and without God in the world.

Ephesians 4:18: Having their understanding darkened, being alienated from the life of God, because of the ignorance that is in them, because of the blindness of their heart;

Colossians 1:21: And you, who once were alienated and enemies in your mind by wicked works, yet now He has reconciled.

James 4:4: Adulterers and adulteresses! Do you not know that friendship with the world is enmity with God? Whoever therefore wants to be a friend of the world makes himself an enemy of God.

God Takes the Initiative in Bringing about Reconciliation.

2 Corinthians 5:18-19: Now all things are of God, who has reconciled us to Himself through Jesus Christ, and has given us the ministry of reconciliation, that is, that God was in Christ reconciling the world to Himself, not imputing their trespasses to them, and has committed to us the word of reconciliation.

Romans 5:6-8: For when we were still without strength, in due time Christ died for the ungodly. For scarcely for a righteous man will one die; yet perhaps for a good man someone would even dare to die. But God demonstrates His own love toward us, in that while we were still sinners, Christ died for us.

Galatians 4:4-5: But when the fullness of the time had come, God sent forth His Son, born of a woman, born under the law, to redeem those who were under the law, that we might receive the adoption as sons.

Ephesians 2:4-5: But God, who is rich in mercy, because of His great love with which He loved us, even when we were dead in trespasses, made us alive together with Christ (by grace you have been saved),

1 John 4:10: In this is love, not that we loved God, but that He loved us and sent His Son to be the propitiation for our sins.

The Means of Reconciliation Is the Death of Jesus Christ.

Romans 5:6: For when we were still without strength, in due time Christ died for the ungodly.

2 Corinthians 5:18-19: Now all things are of God, who has reconciled us to Himself through Jesus Christ, and has given us the ministry of reconciliation, that is, that God was in Christ reconciling the world to Himself, not imputing their trespasses to them, and has committed to us the word of reconciliation.

2 Corinthians 5:21: For He made Him who knew no sin to be sin for us, that we might become the righteousness of God in Him.

Ephesians 2:13: But now in Christ Jesus you who once were far off have been brought near by the blood of Christ.

Ephesians 2:16: And that He might reconcile them both to God in one body through the cross, thereby putting to death the enmity.

Colossians 1:20: And by Him to reconcile all things to Himself, by Him, whether things on earth or things in heaven, having made peace through the blood of His cross.

Group Discussion

1. How can we be better equipped to reach out to people who have lost loved ones to suicide?

2. Does the reality that I have been reconciled to God through Christ make it easier for me to practice the Ministry of presence?

3. Where in the Bible can I identify spiritual resources (prayer, healing, etc.) which can prepare me to help this population of individuals?

Identity Moment

God's resources are endless, and through people in the church community you have help!

Session Four

Question #4: Where can I find hope?

Hope is something that provides us with an invigorating energy which can be contagious! All churches need to be sources and wellsprings of hope for people dealing with despair and depression. The clergy I interviewed indicated that they are ambassadors of hope. The clergy strongly believe that any potential increase in hope and meaning in life may be found in and through such things as religious interventions, observances, and counseling. Feelings of hopelessness can and often may be real for the person left behind through the loss of one who committed suicide. This is a natural reaction, and while it may appear that there is no light in life for them as they are dealing with loss, they have to know that there is hope and help available to them.

The point is that, even when family members may feel a loss of significant hope, they must always remember that no one knows what was going on in the mind of their loved one in the moments prior to their death. Also, calling on the name of the Lord Jesus in the midst of despair always results in a person's salvation. Romans 10:13 states, "For everyone who calls on the name of the Lord shall be saved." There are no ifs, ands, or buts about it or the Word of God is untrue, and we know that this is simply not the case.

Clergy often felt that bereaved people could benefit from the classic congregational setting of a church for a multitude of reasons, "I feel that there's value in attending church services, to being in the presence of God's people who are called to walk the walk of faith with each other, to encourage one another, to be compassionate, to help in whatever way that we can, to hear the Word of God and to be touched by that, to be given the hope that is present in the Word of God."

Compassion breeds hope! Jesus when He looked out on the multitude in Mark 6:34 was moved with compassion.

And Jesus, when he came out, saw much people, and was moved with compassion toward them, because they were as sheep not having a shepherd: and he began to teach them many things (KJV).

Compassion is more than mere empathy or understanding (although it involves those elements); it is a heartfelt, Christ-like movement of love towards another. Compassion breeds hope because it shows the person that you care in a unique way, which they may have never experienced before and need more than ever. It is needed as these individuals are dealing with grief, death, loss, and personal feelings of overwhelming guilt and failure. When one contemplates death, regrets often seep in, questions abound, and doubts about "what ifs" creep in. Indulge me for a moment and imagine today being your last day on earth.

What would you do if you absolutely knew that today was your last day on earth?

- Many might say they would spend it with the family.

- Many might say they would indulge all of their senses; hence, eating, drinking and being merry.

- Many might say they would spend it in solace alone locked in a room somewhere, decrying their life.

- Many might say they would contemplate their mortality

for the first time in their lives, leading to them asking for forgiveness.

One of the hardest things we can do as we face our mortality is to forgive ourselves. We can forgive others, but finally feeling forgiven ourselves may seem like a foreign thought, even if today was the last day of our life.

Forgiveness it not something we can earn or merit. It is a free gift from God in Christ at the cross. We are forgiven and free by accepting what Christ did in our place on the cross. We can then live lives which are truly forgiving to ourselves and to others, as we can only forgive as much as we've been forgiven, and in Christ that's for everything! Much like with funerals, we avoid this topic. We do not want to think about our mortality; we're too busy living and thinking of accumulating more things. The misuse of the phrase "abundant life" is another misnomer of the modern church, often changing the verses of Scripture they use to justify their teachings.

John 10:10 (KJV) says,

> *The thief cometh not, but for to steal, and to kill, and to destroy: I am come that they might have life, and that they might have it more abundantly.*

You see, there's nothing wrong with the word "abundantly." There, it absolutely means "in fullness or overflowing," like the Word says, "pressed down and shaken out." However, the key is a comparison of the devil, the thief who comes to rob us of life. The key in the Greek is the word "life" and what it means. If it merely means biological life, so eat, drink, and be merry for tomorrow we may die, then we should accumulate all we can and engorge ourselves over and over. Christ said He wants this to be something that overflows in our lives through Him.

However, the word in the Greek has nothing to do with bio-logical life, it is "Zoe" life in the Greek, which literally means "life," referring to the principal of life in the spirit and soul. It is distinguished from biological physical life; it is spiritual life.

If you read on in John 10:11 (KJV), Jesus says, "I am the good shepherd: the good shepherd giveth his life for the sheep." The word for life used there is not Zoe life. If Jesus had used that word in verse 10, then we could say eat, drink, and be merry for tomorrow we may die and accumulate all you want. This is because the word He uses in verse 11 regarding laying down His own life is biological life. It literally means "psyche." It is talking about the part of life that man holds in common with the animals.

This is the word for "flesh" which is spoken of regarding the lower region of man's being—what makes him alive as a person or personality. This word is not used in verse 10, but Zoe life is, so the abundant life that Jesus came to give you and me is, indeed, spiritual life as He laid down His own body.

We must realize that a human being is more than an animal. He is more than a body and has more than bodily awareness. A human being, formed in the image of God by God's own hand, is a deathless being who will exist in self-conscious awareness throughout eternity—either with God or separated from Him.

All of our abundant possessions matter not if we do not have abundant life—Zoe life, spiritual life from spiritual death, which is only through Christ! If today was your last day on earth, what matters most? The rich man who wanted to build bigger and bigger barns was just going about life as life is for us, and when it was the last day of his life, he had no idea. Do you need to go out with the Lord now and get right with the

Lord now through Jesus? We all do—make it so! Hope is not far from all of us!

You are a fountain of hope to others! You have hope today! Our loved ones have hope even in death if they had trusted in Christ as their only Savior! Today, we need to place our complete faith in the Lord, whom we can we trust and have hope, assurance, and complete confidence in. We need to be worshipful and ever thankful that we "love Him because He first loved us"[8] and praise Him for initiating His grace in our lives through Christ. We need to heed the call "out of our own lands," laying aside our comfort zones, altars, and worldly ambitions and take the Lord at His Word as we share this hope with these individuals.

We need to trust the fact that we have a hope in Christ and a definite "reason to believe" and allow it to transform our thoughts and shape our hearts and attitudes. We need to uphold and believe the Word of God in the face of stringent opposition and our own complacency. We need to trust that God is who He says He is in His Word and live lives full of expectation and hope that He will ever deliver on His promises, especially in a day and age in which broken promises have become a way of life. You are a fountain of hope right now! Let it flow!

---

[8] I John 4:19.

Discussion Notes

1. What keeps my fountain of hope from flowing?

_____

_____

_____

2. What is abundant life spoken about by Jesus in John 10:10?

_____

_____

_____

3. What would I do for God and others if I knew this was my last day on earth to impact their lives with hope and show them Christ-like compassion?

_____

_____

_____

There are many instances in the Scriptures through which hope can be seen as being directly linked to what we call optimism.

Synopsis: Optimism is the ability to face the future with confidence. For believers this is possible because of their knowledge of God.

Bible Verses Regarding Optimism Resulting From Faith

Confidence in God

Psalm 52:8: But I am like a green olive tree in the house of God; I trust in the mercy of God forever and ever.

Psalm 125:1: Those who trust in the Lord Are like Mount Zion, Which cannot be moved, but abides forever.

Psalm 25:4-5: Show me Your ways, O Lord; Teach me Your paths. Lead me in Your truth and teach me, For You are the God of my salvation; On You I wait all the day.

Psalm 56:4: In God (I will praise His word), In God I have put my trust; I will not fear. What can flesh do to me?

Psalm 71:5: For You are my hope, O Lord God; You are my trust from my youth.

Psalm 91:2: I will say of the Lord, "He is my refuge and my fortress; My God, in Him I will trust."

Nahum 1:7: The Lord is good, A stronghold in the day of trouble; And He knows those who trust in Him.

Confidence in What God Can Do

2 Corinthians 1:10-11: Who delivered us from so great a death, and does deliver us; in whom we trust that He will still deliver us, you also helping together in prayer for us, that thanks may be given by many persons on our behalf for the gift granted to us through many.

Psalm 27:1-3: The Lord is my light and my salvation; Whom shall I fear? The Lord is the strength of my life; Of whom shall I be afraid? When the wicked came against me To eat up my flesh, My enemies and foes, They stumbled and fell. Though an army may encamp against me, My heart shall not fear; Though war may rise against me, In this I will be confident.

Jeremiah 17:7: "Blessed is the man who trusts in the Lord, And whose hope is the Lord."

Micah 7:7: Therefore I will look to the Lord; I will wait for the God of my salvation; My God will hear me.

Hebrews 13:6: So we may boldly say: "The Lord is my helper; I will not fear. What can man do to me?"

1 John 5:14: Now this is the confidence that we have in Him, that if we ask anything according to His will, He hears us.

Confidence in What God Will Do in the Future

2 Corinthians 5:5-8: Now He who has prepared us for this very thing is God, who also has given us the Spirit as a guarantee. So we are always confident, knowing that while we are at home in the body we are absent from the Lord. For we walk by faith, not by sight. We are confident, yes, well pleased rather to be absent from the body and to be present with the Lord.

Acts 24:14-15: But this I confess to you, that according to the Way which they call a sect, so I worship the God of my fathers, believing all things which are written in the Law and in the Prophets. I have hope in God, which they themselves also accept, that there will be a resurrection of the dead, both of the just and the unjust.

Galatians 5:5: For we through the Spirit eagerly wait for the hope of righteousness by faith.

Philippians 1:3-6: I thank my God upon every remembrance of you, always in every prayer of mine making request for you all with joy, for your fellowship in the gospel from the first day until now, being confident of this very thing, that He who has begun a good work in you will complete it until the day of Jesus Christ.

Confidence Founded on God's Grace

Isaiah 12:1-2: And in that day you will say: "O Lord, I will praise You; Though You were angry with me, Your anger is turned away, and You comfort me. Behold, God is my salvation, I will trust and not be afraid; 'For Yah, the Lord, is my strength and song; He also has become my salvation.'"

Ezra 10:2: And Shechaniah the son of Jehiel, one of the sons of Elam, spoke up and said to Ezra, "We have trespassed against our God, and have taken pagan wives from the peoples of the land; yet now there is hope in Israel in spite of this.

2 Corinthians 3:4-5: And we have such trust through Christ toward God. Not that we are sufficient of ourselves to think of anything as being from ourselves, but our sufficiency is from God.

Ephesians 3:12: In whom we have boldness and access with confidence through faith in Him.

2 Thessalonians 2:16-17: Now may our Lord Jesus Christ Himself, and our God and Father, who has loved us and given us everlasting consolation and good hope by grace, comfort your hearts and establish you in every good word and work.

1 John 3:21-22: Beloved, if our heart does not condemn us, we have confidence toward God. And whatever we ask we receive from Him, because we keep His commandments and do those things that are pleasing in His sight.

Group Discussion

1. How can we properly convey hope to the hopeless?

2. How does Christ-like compassion regularly flow from our church and our ministries?

3. What resources /ministries does our church currently have (or not) which display that we are fountains of hope to help this population of individuals? How might we put more on display?

Identity Moment

No matter what life may throw at you, God can give you peace and hope in the middle of any storm.

Session Five

Question #5: Is it my fault?

Self-blame and forgiveness often lead to bitterness, depression, and hopelessness in a person's life. No, it is not your fault! People make their own decisions, and we can never force them to decide one way or the other. I'm going to relate a story to you about a young man who was a Christian, who at one point believed that everything was his fault and wanted to die. This young man felt useless, helpless, and hopeless, and put a gun in his mouth without anyone knowing who was close to him. Although he loved Jesus, he could not feel Him at that moment. When he was ready to pull the trigger, something happened. He closed his eyes and prayed; suddenly, it was as if someone reached in and physically grabbed his heart.

He knew instantly that was the hand of God touching him somewhere that his girlfriend, his parents, his siblings, his friends, and all of his aspirations and hopes could never touch. He slowly removed the gun from his mouth, with tears flowing down his face and cried out to God, "Thank You, Lord! Thank You, Lord."

If he would have taken his life that day, it would have been no one's fault, not the boss who fired him, not the girlfriend who left him, not the mother and father who threatened to disown him, not his sisters who made fun of him, nor his friends who told him he would never amount to anything. It would have been his decision alone.

The ultimate answer to self-blame is assurance that people are individually responsible for their everyday decisions. The clergy interviewed stressed the importance of conveying certain things to survivors and family members who lost loved ones to suicide. One of the main things they stressed was the need for those people to be embraced in their communities, especially religious ones, so that they could receive the support they need for as long as they need it.

Community was important to clergy members in many areas, with one being the necessity of support and comfort that can come from persons with suicidal issues being linked to a community for care. One stated, "That is a responsibility of someone who is the head of a congregation, to make sure that those in the congregation are doing well and, in every capacity, and including the ostracized individual who is depressed and needs other people around them who are spiritually aware."

Another clergy member indicated the following regarding community and networking for support, "I really do believe in a team approach to that. I don't know that one person plays a role that's more primary than anyone else, but I do believe it's a communal problem and so we should handle it is a religious community."

Think about the fact that no matter where you go, you are part of the Body of Christ and the Holy Spirit indwells you. You are part of a living, breathing, sanctified community whether you are at the grocery store or a theme park. This means that you are automatically part of a larger network readily available to support people who suffer from loss, self-blame, and self-hatred. It's more than just inviting people to church, it's reaching out with the hand of grace to show them Christ-like compassion and fill them with truth as you begin to network them into a larger community.

You have the resources in and through community and the

truth of the Word to help people who are dealing with self-blame, and telling them, "It is not your fault!" Sometimes bad things happen in life that are beyond our control, and God allows them to occur perhaps so we can, through suffering, identify with Christ on certain levels and be drawn closer to God. David said in Psalm 119:67-68, "Before I was afflicted I went astray, but now I keep Your word. You are good and do good; teach me Your statutes." The point was that he was suffering and ultimately it drew him closer to God. We suffer in life when we think that we are the cause of someone we love doing harm to themselves, and the pain reverberates as it is a combination of psychological, emotional and physical duress.

I can recall years ago that I had a person in my life who was addicted to drugs. I would give them money, and they would often "pay" me back later with something they would steal from a store. One day they overdosed. I felt complicit, and I knew was my fault. Even though they didn't die, even though I loved them, I was contributing to their demise. It began to wear on me psychologically, mentally, emotionally, and even physically. I had to make a decision: Would I keep on contributing to their substance abuse issue, or would I stop and tell them that I would no longer give them any money?

I loved them and often they threw that in my face. I finally said no, and they didn't really talk to me anymore, which hurt me greatly. What I realize now is that their overdose was not my fault. They had a problem that was rooted in their own decision-making. It's hard when we love someone: we want the best for them, we want them happy, healthy, and alive, but we can't live their lives for them. Ultimately, each individual is responsible for their own decisions (given the fact that they are mentally competent to make them).

Being raised Catholic, it was my understanding and the understanding of my family that suicide was an "unforgivable sin" and any person who committed suicide went straight to hell. This hurt me far worse than the catchy jingles contrived by other kids. It hurt me to know that my brother was now suffering for eternity. There were no remedies for me, no priest or pastors available to help. I felt alone, ashamed, and lost because this was something so unspeakable that I could not share my feelings with anyone because they would not understand.

My life would be forever changed, and my family would be forever changed. People to whom I spoke about this were more than likely already holding pre-conceived notions about suicide, associated with things they had learned through culture, family, and religious circles. Where could I turn for understanding about my brother's supposed suicide? Did anyone understand my grief? Who could help my mother, father, and the rest of my family? Ultimately, was it my fault?

Later in life, after I was saved and in a church community, I began to gain a fuller understanding of the grace and forgiveness of the Lord, which helped to erase my feeling of self-blame, self-hatred, and guilt over it being my fault. Through community and the truth which you have, people who live lives isolated in hatred, loss, and guilt (who are all around us) can be transformed by the overwhelming grace of God. You telling them that it isn't their fault may not initially be enough, but gradually assimilating them into the truth of forgiveness found only in Jesus is more than enough. Share your story. Share your testimony. Tell them of how Christ saved you and how being part of God's community helps you deal with your own encounters with self-blame and brings God's gracious hand to your sufferings.

Discussion Notes

1. What has helped you overcome self-blame in your own spiritual walk?

_____

_____

_____

2. What is the essence of a church community?

_____

_____

_____

3. How do you relate to the sufferings of Christ? How do His sufferings impact your own?

_____

_____

_____

There are many instances in Scriptures dealing with suffering.

Basis for Suffering

Synopsis: Believers ought to expect to suffer as an inevitable part of their calling. To believe is not to evade suffering; it is to face it with new confidence and hope. Rightly approached, suffering develops the character of believers, equips them for more effective service, draws believers closer to Jesus Christ, and prepares them for eternal life.

Reasons Why Believers Must Expect Suffering:

- Jesus Christ foretold it
- The Apostles foretold it
- The experience of the Old Testament shows it
- The experience of the New Testament shows it
- Suffering for Jesus Christ is commendable
- Suffering is profitable
- It affirms believers' adoption
- It is the price of Godliness
- It is a condition of service
- It develops trust
- It develops character
- It deepens fellowship
- It draws believers to the Lord
- It prepares believers for heaven

There are many encouragements in Scripture for us when we suffer which will help us to get through it!

Synopsis: Believers are encouraged by the loving care and faithful promises of God and by the example, support and prayers of fellow believers. The prospect of heaven helps them to endure.

- The encouragement of God's love
- The care of the Father
- The sympathetic understanding of Jesus Christ
- The comfort of the Spirit
- The promises of God
- The encouragement of the fellowship of believers
- Examples from the past
- Support from other believers
- The encouragement of looking ahead
- The assurance of victory
- The prospect of glory

Bible Verses Regarding Suffering and Encouragement

Reasons why believers must expect suffering:

Jesus Christ Foretold It

Matthew 10:22: And you will be hated by all for My name's sake. But he who endures to the end will be saved.

Matthew 10:17: But beware of men, for they will deliver you up to councils and scourge you in their synagogues.

Matthew 23:34: Therefore, indeed, I send you prophets, wise men, and scribes: some of them you will kill and crucify, and some of them you will scourge in your synagogues and persecute from city to city,

Matthew 24:9: "Then they will deliver you up to tribulation and kill you, and you will be hated by all nations for My name's sake.

Luke 21:16-17: You will be betrayed even by parents and brothers, relatives and friends; and they will put some of you to death. And you will be hated by all for My name's sake.

The Apostles Foretold It

Acts 14:22: Strengthening the souls of the disciples, exhorting them to continue in the faith, and saying, "We must through many tribulations enter the kingdom of God."

2 Timothy 3:12: Yes, and all who desire to live godly in Christ Jesus will suffer persecution.

Philippians 1:29: For to you it has been granted on behalf of Christ, not only to believe in Him, but also to suffer for His sake,

1 John 3:13: Do not marvel, my brethren, if the world hates you.

Revelation 2:10: Do not fear any of those things which you are about to suffer. Indeed, the devil is about to throw some of you into prison, that you may be tested, and you will have tribulation ten days. Be faithful until death, and I will give you the crown of life.

Group Discussion

1. Define suffering.

2. Define community.

3. Define forgiveness.

Identity Moment

In following Christ, you can be assured that He will help you to endure hardships.

Concluding Thoughts and Challenge!

What can we say? That indeed we do have answers to the five most common questions that people ask clergy about when someone they love takes their life.

Here's the list again:

1. Is my loved one in hell?

2. Is suicide the "unforgivable sin"?

3. How can the church help me?

4. Where can I find hope?

5. Is it my fault?

Answers We Have (Synopsis):

If your loved one believed in Jesus (trusted and relied exclusively on Jesus Christ as their Savior) before their death, there is no way that they are in hell, but rather are now in God's presence in heaven. No ecclesiastical body, no supposed religious expert, no prognosticator or soothsayer, no friend, relative or Bible scholar can definitively tell you otherwise. Suicide is not the unforgivable, the unpardonable sin. We have no idea what was going through a person's mind in the moments before their death.

No, suicide is not the unforgivable sin. Blasphemy of the Holy Spirit is the unforgivable sin. If you are still open to receiving Jesus as your Savior, then you have not committed blasphemy of the Holy Spirit!

The church has resources to help you, clergy members are ready to help you, and church members that you know should be willing to help you. The church has many spiritual resources and the clergy interviewed here have indicated that they are willing to liaise with the community and find even more resources for you.

You can find hope through Jesus Christ. You can find hope through men and women of faith in the clergy who care about you and are ready, willing, and able to be present with you in your time of suffering.

No, it is not your fault. People make their own choices, and we cannot own their choices and the consequences of their actions. We can only try to help them the best way we know how and that's through the Living Word (Jesus) and the written word of truth!

Challenge!

That we will live out the reality of what the Word of God says about suicide and open our lives and church ministries to help survivors.

That people who have lost loved ones to suicide have assurance and hope in the here and now. No matter what society says to them, what friends and family may say, or what is rooted in their minds because they have heard it over and over, they have hope!

As you read and re-read the chapters associated with the Identity Moments, ponder on the words of Scripture that have been presented and then read the words of the clergy. I promise you that if you do this with a clear mind, seeking the truth, and if you let the truth of Christ which has been presented penetrate your mind, will, and heart, you will be able to receive assurance and hope today!

The challenge is to pass it on and be a fountain of hope for others!

Do you accept it?

Bibliography

A. J. Droge, A. J. "Suicide," ed. David Noel Freedman. *The Anchor Yale Bible Dictionary* (New York: Doubleday, 1992).

Lane, William L. *The Gospel of Mark* (Wm. B. Eerdmans Publishing, 1974).

Contact information:

Internet:
https://connect-the-dots-ministries.ueniweb.com/

To order online:
https://connect-the-dots-ministries.ueniweb.com/
products/books/suicide-unforgivable-51715322

Email: tperchitti@aol.com

Contact@connectthedotsministry.com

About the Author

THOMAS PERCHITTI (ED. d) is a family man who has been married to Ivy Dianne Perchitti since 1993. They have three boys, Michael (26), Christopher (22), and Jonathan (19). Michael is married to Victorria, and they have two daughters, Giada and Elena.

Dr. Perchitti has been an ordained minister since 2005 and has served as senior pastor of Tyre Ref. Church since 2012. He is also an NAMB endorsed Army Chaplain (2011) (IRR). This is Dr. Perchitti's first book, and he hopes that the grace and compassion of Christ can be shown in and through the work.

www.ingramcontent.com/pod-product-compliance
Lightning Source LLC
Chambersburg PA
CBHW070941120626
46546CB00004B/1513